My God is so big

Written by Catherine Mackenzie

Illustrated by Andy Robb

CF4·K

My God is So Big

My God is so big, so strong and so migh-ty, There's no-thing that He can-not do.

The ri-vers are His, the moun-tains are His, The stars are His han-di-work too.

My God is so big, so strong and so migh-ty, There's noth-ing that He can-not do.

Music layout: Ewen Ritchie © copyright words: public domain

My God is so big,
so strong and so mighty.
There's nothing that he cannot do.
My God is so big,
so strong and so mighty.
There's nothing that he cannot do.
The mountains are his,
the rivers are his,
the stars are his handiwork too.
My God is so big,
so strong and so mighty.
There's nothing that he cannot do
for me, for you,
that's true.

God is so **big** .... He's **bigger** than you and he's bigger than me.

God's bigger than everybody.

He's **bigger** than the elephant that he created and the mountains that he made.

SCOOOSSSHH

SWOOOOSSHH

He's **bigger** than the ocean that he filled with fish and the sky that he filled with birds and clouds.

God is so **big** that you can't even measure him. You can't put him in a box or even in a building. He is everywhere, all the time.

He's so **big** – he created the whole of outer space. All the planets, stars and galaxies – even the ones that we haven't found yet.

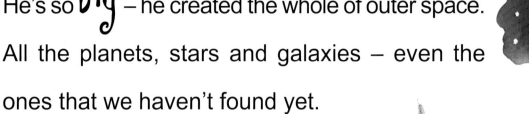

He is so B I G.

My God is so **big** that he knows everything. He knows about ants and worms and creepy crawlies. He doesn't forget about them.

creeepy creep

flutter flutter

God is so **big** that he sees everything. He doesn't need a microscope to see tiny things.

My God is so big that he can even see your thoughts and feelings, even when you try to hide them. Your mum or dad might think that they know what you are thinking about.

flutter   flutter

But they can never know for sure. You can be saying one thing with your mouth but thinking something else in your head.

But our God is so big that he even knows the thoughts inside your head. Your best friend might think that they know everything about you.

But there are some things that you keep to yourself. There are some things you keep secret. But God can see all of that.

My God is so **big** that he even knows the thoughts in your mind and the feelings of your heart.

When you feel **angry** with someone, God knows.
When you feel *jealous* of your friend, God knows.

When you feel **sad** because you are lonely, God knows.
When you are feeling **HAPPY** because you love God,
God knows that too.

God is so **big** that he sees everything you do. God can see behind closed doors and he can see in the dark.

Even if you wore the greatest disguise that ever was so that even your own granny wouldn't recognise you, God would know exactly who you were. You can't hide from him.

God is so **big** that he knows all that there is to know. He knows if you are helpful or unhelpful, friendly or unfriendly, obedient or disobedient.

God knows if you believe in him or not. He knows if you love him or if you don't. He knows if you obey him or if you don't.

God is so big… yet, he can live inside you if you ask him to. If you thank Jesus Christ for dying for you and ask God to forgive your sins, then God will send his Holy Spirit to you.

He will be your friend and live inside you. You will then be part of God's family.

My God is so **big** that he can be with all of his people, all of the time, anywhere and everywhere! Isn't he amazing!

My God is so **strong**. He is stronger than lions. They pounce and roar and attack. Other animals are afraid of them. But lions are not stronger than God.

Lions get their food from God. They depend on him. God is so **strong** that even lions do what he tells them to do. Daniel was thrown into a lions' den, but the lions couldn't touch him. God sent an angel to close their mouths.

My God is so **strong**. He can even walk across water!

That's true!

It really is!

Can you walk across water? No, you can't! Water is dangerous and if you fall in it you could drown.

But our God is stronger than us and stronger than the churning oceans. Just one word from God and the oceans obey him.

Jesus told the waves to be quiet and the wind to stop. They obeyed him. Jesus walked right across the water. His friends, the disciples, saw him and were amazed.

My God is so **strong**. He is stronger than the strongest man. Samson was strong. God used him to defeat the Philistines.

But Samson still wasn't stronger than God. No one is.

God made people. But people do not last for ever. Every person has to die some day. Some get sick and need looking after.

People can't live for ever.

But God is so **strong** – he lasts for ever, he is eternal.

God is so **MIGHTY.** He can even stop sickness.

When Jesus was on earth he cured the sick, made blind people see and lame people able to leap, run and jump all over the place.

We should all sing praises to God and shout about how he is wonderful and brilliant and **MIGHTY!**

God is so **MIGHTY** that he can change you. God can make you more like Jesus.

God can help you to obey him and love him. God makes you into a new person.

That is amazing.

That is **MIGHTY!**

God is so **MIGHTY** he even destroyed death.

When Jesus died... three days later he came back to life.

He's so **MIGHTY!**

If you ask God to forgive you he will forgive you.

God will give you eternal life so that when you die you can come to heaven to live with him instead.

My God is so *big*, so **strong** and so **MIGHTY**.

My God is so **big**, so **strong** and so **MIGHTY**.

Everything is under God's control. Think about the millions of people in the world. God knows all about them.

He even knows the day when they will die and meet him face to face.

God never gets sleepy. Every morning you wake up, but in a few hours time you go to sleep again. God doesn't need sleep.

He is always awake.

Sometimes you have great fun on your holidays.

But God is so *big* and so **strong** and so **MIGHTY** that he never takes a holiday.

God never stops loving his people.

God loves them too much for that.

His love is just so **big** … it has no end.

God knows what he is doing. He is always ready.

My God is so big, **strong** and **MIGHTY!**.

He is the organiser of the world. He is in control.

Every year has seasons. In the spring plants start to grow. In the summer trees grow fresh fruit to eat. In the autumn the leaves fall and then in the winter the cold weather comes.

This has happened every year since you were born. It has happened every year since your grandmother was born. For thousands of years, seasons have come and gone because God is always working and taking care of things.

My God is so *big*

and so **strong**

and so **MIGHTY!**

Everything belongs to him!

All the mountains, rivers, plants and animals belong to God. God made them. They were his idea and he cares for them. He wants us to care for them too.

But there's one thing he wants us to do most of all... and that's love him, obey him and ...

Praise his name for ever....

If you love Jesus it isn't possible to imagine all the wonderful things that he will do for you. But the most wonderful thing will be going to live with Jesus one day.

My God is so big and so **strong** and so MIGHTY...
My God can do anything!

Do you like going home at the end of a busy day? One day, if you love Jesus, he will take you to live with him in his home. His home is called Heaven.

Heaven is such a magnificent, incredible, amazing, joyful, perfect, awesome place... you'll just love it!

Every corner is perfect because **Jesus Christ** made it. Every moment that you spend there will be beautiful because he will be there with you.

My God is so *big* and so **strong** and so **MIGHTY**.

There's nothing that he cannot do for me or for you, THAT'S TRUE!

So now you know that God is so big so strong and so mighty... read these verses in the Bible which prove that he is.

Psalm 77:13-16

Who is so great a God as our God? You are the God who does wonders; you have declared your strength among the peoples. You have with your arm redeemed your people, the sons of Jacob and Joseph. The waters saw You, O God;
The waters saw You, they were afraid. The depths also trembled.

Matthew 9:6

Jesus has power to forgive sins.

Psalm 18:1-2

I will love you O Lord my strength.
The Lord is my rock and my fortress and my deliverer.

Psalm 46:1

God is our refuge and strength, he is always ready to help in times of trouble. Therefore we will not be afraid even though the earth shakes and the mountains crash into the sea.

Psalm 24:8;10

Who is this King of glory? The Lord strong and mighty ...
The Lord of hosts, he is the King of glory.

Ephesians 6:10

Be strong in the Lord and in the power of his might.

This book is written for Lydia, Esther, Philip, Lois, Jack, Marianne, Isobel, Elizabeth and for children just like them. CMM

© Copyright 2002 Christian Focus Publications. Reprinted 2013. ISBN: 978-1-78191-134-1.
Published by Christian Focus Publications, Geanies House, Fearn, Tain, Ross-shire, IV20 1TW, Scotland.
www.christianfocus.com email:info@christianfocus.com. Illustrations: Andy Robb, Cover design: C Mackenzie.
Printed in China